THE NETWORK MARKETING HANDBOOK
Goal: To Attract Great Clients to Your Business

Please start by answering these questions:

1. What is your 30 second elevator pitch?

2. How do you primarily service your clients?

3. What are you currently doing to market your business?

4. Non-profits - who are your funding sources?

What Is Marketing?

MARKETING IS EVERYTHING you do to promote your business, from the moment you conceive of it, to the point at which customers buy your product or service and begin to patronize your business on a regular basis. The key words to remember are everything and regular basis.

The meaning is clear: Marketing includes the name of your business, the determination of whether you will be selling a product or service, the method of manufacture or servicing, the colors, size, and shape of your product, the packaging, the location of your business, the advertising, the public relations, the sales training, the sales presentation, the telephone inquiries, the problem solving, the growth plan, the referral plan and the follow-up. If you gather from this that marketing is a complex process, you're right.

See marketing as a circle that starts with your idea for generating revenue and completes itself when you have the blessed patronage of repeat and referral business. If your marketing is not a circle, it's a straight line that leads right to the bankruptcy courts. - *From Guerrilla Marketing, 3rd Edition by Jay Conrad Levinson*

Marketing is belief in yourself transferred to someone else. - *First heard from Suliaman Rahman, President of the Greater Philadelphia African American Chamber of Commerce*

Marketing is ultimately service. This has been a great definition for nearly 40 years. This definition clearly provides the focus needed by both local and national companies when seeking sustainable success. While marketing has traditionally meant advertising to many, advertising alone does not mean success. - *Excerpts from the book "American Business Ownership Development - In God We Trust"*

NEWMAN/NETWORKS

7 Steps to a Highly Effective Marketing Plan

Most business owners are DOERS not PLANNERS!

An example: One summer my husband, Roy and I decided to travel by car to California. We live outside of Nashville, TN. We wanted to see the sights and arrive in San Francisco. We knew that California was West of Tennessee and that since Memphis is West of Nashville, we took Interstate 40 West to Memphis.

Shortly outside of Memphis I looked up and saw a sign, New Orleans, 250 miles.

"What?" I shouted. "New Orleans? What are you doing?" To which Roy replied, "I picked up information at our last stop on a really great package plan that includes gasoline for $.99 a gallon, buy one get one free dinner, and a free continental breakfast. All of this with the hotel room for only $89 a night. I didn't see how we could go wrong."

"Is this the right way?" I asked.

"Check, the map." He replied.

At that point we both realized we thought the other one would pick up the map before leaving home. Oh well, no one could deny that this was a great package with a hotel room in New Orleans. We were on the way to successfully reaching California.

After spending the next morning in New Orleans we again headed West. Outside of Baton Rouge a friend called us on the cell phone and said that she had been reading the Bargain Hunter's Digest "List of Must Do". There was a place in San Antonio that was having the biggest "Sale in History." Since she knew that we were on our way to California she thought we would want to spend a day at this phenomenal sale. Of course she was right. When I

mentioned it to Roy, he wanted to know if San Antonio was on the way to San Francisco.

"Well, the sign says West to Houston." I said. "I know Houston is in Texas. San Antonio is in Texas, so it must be. I'll ask the attendant when we stop to get gas how far it is."

"Should we stop and find a map?" Roy wanted to know. We talked it over, and decided since we knew that we were heading West, since we were already going 70 miles an hour, and since we were finding such great deals, why should we waste time, money, and effort in finding a map.

Sound crazy? ABSOLUTELY you say. And yet, this is exactly how most businesses are run. They have a product (like the trip in the story) and they want to earn a living and even become financially independent (San Francisco). They know they are getting there, because they are making more money now than when they started (for us, we knew because the signs kept indicating West).

Yet, is this the quickest, most effective, least expensive way to grow the business? Well the business owner is going 70 miles an hour, the advertising is a great deal, or some friend tells them they should add a certain product to increase sales; so they never STOP and take the time and effort to BUY A MAP. In other words, they never DEVELOP AN EFFECTIVE MARKETING PLAN.

Did we eventually reach San Francisco? Yes, we could have. Roy says it is important to let you know this is not a true story – He would never travel without a map. This would be a wonderful trip if time, money, and effort were bountiful. Will you make your goals in your business without a plan? Probably. However, if you want to build a successful business in less time, less effort, and use less money to do so, DEVELOP AN EFFECTIVE MARKETING PLAN.

NEWMAN/NETWORKS

This is a story about my visit to PFCU on Tuesday, July 5th.

As I stood in line at the bank yesterday, the gentleman behind me said "I get terrible service at this bank." I replied "I have not gotten that same feedback." He then replied, "You need to get out more, when I go to the banks in Springfield, they greet me by my first name." I replied "They do the same thing to me here. But I am here at least once a week." He said "Those banks know me by my first name." I asked "Do you know the tellers here by their first name? I do." He replied "No, I don't have to." I thought to myself – Well, there is your answer.

I have been a member of the credit union for over 16 years. I receive great customer service because I **GIVE** great customer service. I know the tellers by their first name and try to be an accommodating PFCU member. As the gentleman and I discussed the situation further, I found out where we disagree. In his opinion, the best support is investing financially (buying real estate, making deposits, etc.) in the community. In my opinion, the best support is showing up. While it is true that time and money are both limited assets, the most limiting is time. I spend the time to hone my relationships. While email, text and Facebook messages are great, people feel most valued when you are standing in front of them.

Think about how you value not only your customers but your employees (WHO are your business) and your business partners (including your bank!) Because marketing ultimately is SERVICE!

Outline of the 7 Steps to a
Highly Effective Marketing Plan

Goal for this Outline: Facilitate and lead you into developing a plan to use in marketing your business. You can add to, enhance and improve as you go forward.

Purpose: To increase your profitability.

Step 1: Clearly define your product.

Step 2: Determine your best customer.

Step 3: What is unique about the way you do business? Why should your customer buy from you?

Step 4: What is your message?

Step 5: Ways to get your message to your best customer?

Step 6: What are your Marketing Goals?

Step 7: Develop a calendar and a budget.

Two things to remember:

1. Marketing plans don't work! You work the marketing plan.

Whether this means you or your marketing staff, marketing is a "to do" that is an integral part of a growing, successful business.

2. Results must be measured!

Whatever you do, find a way to measure results. How many new customers did you bring in as a result of this effort? How did sales increase?

Step 1: Clearly define your product.

1. Do people buy what they need or do they buy what they want?

People buy what they want. They use justifications to convince themselves they need the things they want. Agree?

2. What is/are your products?

3. What service do you provide?

4. When is this needed?

5. What purpose does this product serve?

Step 2: Determine your best customer.

KNOWING your customer intimately is the first step to MORE sales, EASIER sales and LARGER sales.

1. Know WHO your customers **(people you serve and funding sources)** are.

2. Know WHAT your customers want.

3. Know what MOTIVATES your customer to buy.

To really get to know your customers answer these questions:

1. How does your potential customer normally buy similar products?

Case study: Elizabeth realized that over the last three years, her clients came from referrals from nursing homes, estate attorneys, and former clients.

2. How have your clients come to you?

3. How do they decide to use your services?

4. If your business is new, how do people in general choose your product or service?

5. Who are the primary buyer and the primary buying influencer in the purchasing process?

6. What kind of habits does your customer have? (For instance, where do they get their information?)

Case study: Elizabeth realized that it would be beneficial to hold seminars about holistic medicine and the alternative types of treatment in Centers devoted to Aging. She found that people using her service wanted to be educated about all the alternatives available.

Step 2: Determine your best customer. (Continued)

7. What are your target customer's primary motivations for buying (i.e. to look good, avoid pain, get rich, be healthy, be popular, etc.)?

a. Your ideal customer is:

b. That client reads the following:

c. They attend:

d. They make decisions:

Step 3: What is unique about the way you do business?
Pick a Niché or Declare a Unique Selling Proposition

1. If you say that your target customer is EVERYBODY then NOBODY will be your customer. *Example: Which speaker would you hire first? The one that told you he could speak about anything. Or the one that told you she only gives speeches on writing an effective marketing plan? Most people would rather hear the expert.*

2. The marketplace is jam packed with COMPETITION, with ADVERTISING and with PRODUCTS. Set yourself APART from your COMPETITION.

BECOME AN EXPERT! BECOME AN EXPERT! BECOME AN EXPERT!

Example: *Case study: Elizabeth only provides care for the elderly using holistic, alternative treatments. She is not a home health agency. She does go to the home. She sets her company apart with WHAT she does.*

What are some other examples of experts, specialists, etc.?

3. There are many ways to define a niché or a Unique Selling Proposition. While there is a distinction between these two, I tend to use them interchangeably. The importance is to differentiate your business.

What is unique about the way you do business?

Step 4: What is your message?
Develop Your Marketing Message

Your marketing message not only tells your prospect what you offer, but convinces them you are the best or the only business to provide this to them.

1. Answer in less than 15 words, "What do you do?"

2. List phrases and statements describing your business, your best customers, and what is unique about the way you do business.

3. Choose the best of these phrases to use in your marketing.

Step 5: Ways to get your message to your best customers.
The following is a list of ways to market our business

Weapon	Audience	Using Well	Using - Needs Work	Not Using But Should	Not Appropriate
1. Newspaper ads					
2. Contests					
3. Card decks					
4. Posters					
5. Seminars					
6. Television ads					
7. Signs					
8. Sweepstakes					
9. Door-to-door					
10. Teleclasses					
11. Radio ads					
12. Banners					
13. Tradeshows					
14. Yellow pages					
15. Articles					
16. Classified ads					
17. Newsletter					
18. Charity events					

Weapon	Audience	Using Well	Using - Needs Work	Not Using But Should	Not Appropriate
19. Networking					
20. Infomercials					
21. Billboards					
22. Take-one box					
23. Telemarketing					
24. Magazine ads					
25. Special events					
26. Sales letters					
27. Flyers					
28. Emails					
29. Movie ads					
30. Ezine ads					
31. Postcards					
32. Door hangers					
33. Agents					
34. Media releases					
35. Fax broadcasts					
36. Brochures					
35. Fax broadcasts					
36. Brochures					

37. Gift certificates					
38. Word-of-mouth					
39. Website					
40. Sign picketing					
41. Business cards					
42. Catalogs					
43. Air blimps					
44. Public speaking					

Weapon	Audience	Using Well	Using - Needs Work	Not Using But Should	Not Appropriate
45. Window display					
46. Serve on an association board					
47. Charity fundraisers					
48. Reprints					
49. 800 Number					
50. Targeted list					
51. Audio and videotapes					
52. Refreshments offered					

53. Credit cards					
54. Effective use of voicemail					
55. Circulars					
56. Pricing					
57. Phone on-hold marketing					
58. Research studies					
59. Make an audio tape					
60. Waiting room resources					
61. Customer Reactivation Letter					
62. Free Consultation					
Weapon	*Audience*	*Using Well*	*Using - Needs Work*	*Not Using But Should*	*Not Appropriate*
63. Logo					
64. Promo Kit					
65. Stationery					
66. Testimonials					
67. Marketing Plan					

NEWMAN NETWORKS

Choose the top 5 to 10 weapons you will use for the Big To Do List:

1. _____
2. _____
3. _____
4. _____
5. _____
6. _____
7. _____
8. _____
9. _____
10. _____

Choose the 2 to 4 that you will use monthly:

1. _____

2. _____

3. _____

4. _____

Step 6: What are your marketing goals?

Set S M A R T goals:

S ensible

M easurable

A chievable

R ealistic

T angible

Goals should include: Financial elements, such as amount of income, number of sales and amount of profit. Non-financial elements, such as books you will read, networking events to attend and number of articles published.

Bottom Line:

What are your 3 top goals for this marketing campaign?

1. _____

2. _____

3. _____

Step 7: Develop a calendar and budget.

This is the step where you plan your attack. You begin to take action.

1. Take a calendar. I like to use a google calendar. Schedule your activities on your calendar.

2. Plan a budget based on these activities.

3. Keep track of your effectiveness:

a. What is working, continue.

b. What is not working, change a little.

c. If it still does not work, do something new.

Step 8: Develop a calendar and budget for social media.

Limiting Factors: Manpower _____

Limiting Factors: Budget _____

Social Media Sites	Audience	Goal	Content	Posting Cycle	Budget
Facebook					
Linkedin					
YouTube					
Twitter					
Foursquare					

NEWMAN NETWORKS

Step 8: Develop a calendar and budget for social media. (Continued)

Social media websites have a different audience and might require a small tweak in your approach. Each site should have a strategy. *For example - The Newman Networks strategy for Facebook is to reach new customers through friends of friends. The Linkedin strategy is to stay in touch with potential customers and sponsors The Youtube strategy is to develop content.*

1. Marketing Strategy for Facebook.

2. Marketing Strategy for Twitter.

3. Marketing Strategy for YouTube.

4. Marketing Strategy for Linkedin.

5. Marketing Strategy for your Website.

Resources:

All inclusive site, developed by Constant Contact, dedicated to providing how-to instructions for using social media sites.
http://www.socialquickstarter.com/

Source for searching the entire World Wide Web for mentions of your company or another business (i.e. competitor) http://www.socialmention.com/

Yellow pages for Twitter. Allows you to search for real-time conversations about a particular subject. http://www.twellow.com/

Constant Contact Resource: allows consolidation of all email alerts from most social media sites. http://nutshellmail.com/

Dashboard for scheduling "sends" or "posts" through social media sites.
http://hootsuite.com/

Latest tools: http://www.mashable.com

NEWMAN NETWORKS

NOTES

Biography:

Nicole Newman is an inspiring motivational writer, public speaker and business networker. She was born in Washington DC and grew up in the City of Brotherly Love, Philadelphia. A product of Julia R. Reynolds Masterman School and the High School of Engineering and Science, she acquired a strong work ethic. She started her college career at the University of North Carolina at Greensboro. Although she was unable to complete school at the University of NC at Greensboro, 2 months later while on crutches she transferred to Temple University and graduate Magna Cum Laude from the Fox School of Business with a Bachelors of Business Administration in Risk Management and Insurance, Management Information Systems and a minor in Human Resources. She went on to complete her MBA at the prestigious Robert H. Smith School of Business at the University of Maryland majoring in Finance.

Nicole started her company, Newman Networks in April of 2006 which owned www.diversephilly.com, a website for businesses to share the costs of advertising. In just the second year, the company quadrupled revenue. With 2000 linkedin connections, 8000 facebook friends and 80 testimonials, the company created a massive network in the local marketplace. This is just one of the testimonials – *"Nicole Newman is an outstanding individual. She is an incredible connector and exemplifies in her daily life the proof that networking is the key to building a successful business. Nicole cares most about her clients, colleagues and friends; assisting them in building strong relationships that will lead to company growth and success. Anyone doing business in the Greater Philadelphia region should get to know Nicole immediately. She will absolutely take your business to the next level."* from Kate Bay, Regional Account Executive, Greater Philadelphia Chamber of Commerce.

Nicole is a former member of the Greater Philadelphia Chamber of Commerce, and was recently honored with Urban Momentum's 2009 Networker of the Year. She has won the Count Me In Make Mine a Million $ Pitch Competition in 2010. She is one of the 2013 winner of the NAACP's 101 Influential African American Women in Philadelphia.

NEWMAN NETWORKS

www.ingramcontent.com/pod-product-compliance
Lightning Source LLC
Chambersburg PA
CBHW051235200326
41519CB00025B/7391